How to Grow Rich with The Millionaire Mind Script

By

Praveen Kumar & Prashant Kumar

Terms of Use

Disclaimer

The advice contained in this material might not be suitable for everyone. The author obtained the information from sources believed to be reliable and from his own personal experience, but he neither implies nor intends any guarantee of accuracy.

The author, publisher and distributors never give legal, accounting, medical or any other type of professional advice. The reader must always seek those services from competent professionals that can review their own particular circumstances.

The author, publisher and distributors particularly disclaim any liability, loss, or risk taken by individuals who directly or indirectly act on the information contained herein. All readers must accept full responsibility for their use of this material.

All pictures used in this book are for illustrative purposes only. The people in the pictures are not connected with the book, author or publisher and no link or endorsement between any of them and the topic or content is implied, nor should any be assumed. The pictures are only licensed for use in this book and must not be used for any other purpose without prior written permission of the rights holder. ˙

Table of Contents

Table of Contents

Introduction

The first step to becoming an enlightened millionaire is to get the mindset of a millionaire. **Process of wealth creation is 90% psychology and only 10% strategy**. Most people fail to become rich because they want to learn the strategy and not focus on changing their psychology.

To be a winner, you have to have the mindset of a winner. The inner change has to precede the external outcome. We have known this since the time we were kids: a certain set of rules enlisted by our parents, teachers and peers need to be followed. We believed in them because they were given to us in love and in good faith. Some of the rules that were ingrained in us were from people whose mindsets were steeped in poverty. We can't blame them because one or two generations back, most of our families were poor and struggling to survive.

As the world moves towards greater prosperity, we have to learn the new set of rules that govern the rich. The new rules are easy to learn only if you have an open mind to learn and succeed. We have to rewrite the script, or order a new set of rules that govern our lives.

It is not sufficient to get rid of the old impressions from our minds – it is only the first step. The old script was a baggage that held us back from becoming rich and forbade us from living life to its full potential.

To succeed, we have to re-write the old script to that of the 'Enlightened Millionaire' in our minds. This is the inner principle of wealth creation. Once the new script is written, it is a point of no return. You can never be middle-class or poor again even if you lose your entire wealth and have to restart from a scratch.

The millionaire mindset once achieved, is a non-destructive commodity. It stays with you for life. You can lose your millions but you will always bounce back. You are a millionaire because of your mindset.

Re-write the Script

The motivation to re-write the script has to originate from the heart because the mind has its own set of limitations— it is always the heart that rules. Whenever there is a conflict between the heart and the mind, it is always the heart that wins. A transformational change can occur only if it comes from the heart. Incremental increase of knowledge can take place in the mind but transformation of the mind can take place only if the heart is involved.

The heart, as we know it, is our subconscious. How can we involve our subconscious into the wealth creation process? To do that, we have to understand what triggers our heart and soul. We have so many desires buried within our subconscious. We have to simply uncover and trigger one or more of these desires into the wealth creation process.

To involve the heart means to find the predominant motivating triggers and activating them. You cannot live someone else's dream— you have to find your own.

The secret of wealth creation lies in finding your own triggers that drive your heart and soul. The nobler your trigger, the greater are your chances of success. A higher and better cause gets more people involved and your chances towards success increases exponentially.

A callous desire normally results in conflicting situations with a lesser chance of success. However, there is nothing wrong in following any of your dreams because once a dream is satisfied; there is always a next dream that will trigger you towards greater cause and effect. It is an evolutionary process. It is however, prudent on what you set your heart on and as Emerson rightly pointed out, "*it surely will be yours.*"

To understand our triggers, we have to apply the *S.S.S* formula explained by Ron Holland in his book Talk and Grow Rich. According to him, to understand our subconscious we have to follow **SILENCE, STILLNESS AND SOLITUDE**. The secret to understanding these triggers of our mind lies in meditation – in silence, stillness and solitude or the S.S.S. When you become quiet, it just dawns on you.

Sometimes, an external stimulus is needed to activate the internal process... much like the process of falling in love. It is the beauty of an external person that activates love and desire in our hearts.

Similarly, experience of suffering can ignite compassion in our hearts. At times by putting ourselves in situations and gaining the right stimuli, we can understand the triggers that operate within our subconscious.

You will be able to re-write the '**enlightened millionaire**' script much faster if you understand your dreams and inner motivation. So take time out to understand these dreams and write them on a piece of paper—it will hasten the process. If you know your objective, then the path to success becomes easier to tread on.

The Butterfly Effect

To bring about internal change in our attitude, we have to understand the butterfly effect. The phrase refers to the idea that the flapping of a butterfly's wings might create tiny changes in the atmosphere that ultimately cause a tornado to appear (or prevent a tornado from appearing.)

The flapping wing represents a small change in the initial condition of the system, which causes a chain of events leading to large-scale phenomena. This implies that a small change in the initial condition may produce large variations in the long-term behavior of the system.

We do not have to do anything spectacular to help change our script to an 'enlightened millionaire's mindset,' but we can make small changes to alter the initial condition that can change the long term trajectory of our lives. In the succeeding paragraphs we will discuss some suggestions that can trigger a butterfly effect. You may apply some or all of them to change the outcome of your life.

Controlling the Inputs to Your Mind

To change the script of our life, we have to understand how the script is written in the mind. The script in the mind is written through thoughts, words, feelings and actions. Each one of them is very important as they leave indelible impressions on the mind. If we can learn to control our thoughts, words, feelings and actions in the present, then we have the power to change our future.

Power of Thoughts and Words

Thoughts are subtle but important because they are the starting point of the process. But once they become words, they have tremendous impact on both our internal and external reality. If you don't believe me, just call someone a bastard and your teeth will come out. Similarly, words of love and kindness will evoke a totally different – but positive – response.

Words, both written and oral, have tremendous power. They leave a deep impression on the mind. We are responsible for our thoughts and words and have to learn to control them. To have the millionaire's mindset, we have to snap out of any negative thought or action.

We have to read or listen to the words of successful and enlightened wealth creators. We have to place ourselves in their company and associate with them so that their words may influence us and change our script.

To illustrate this point: write down the names of five people with whom you spend your maximum time. Now, study their profile. Are they rich...

entrepreneurs? Are they wealth creators? Or are they limited in their vision of job security? If you hang around with poor, negative and unsuccessful people then that is what the future beholds for you. You are writing the script of poverty.

To write the script of an enlightened wealth creator, you have to seek the right company to influence your mind. You have to change your reading habits and listen to lectures and tapes of highly successful people. You have to learn to speak the language of the rich.

Your script change will gain added momentum when words of success and positivity start flowing from your pen and mouth. The words you think, write and speak have greater impact on your mind than the words you receive from others.

Initially, the control of thoughts and words will look artificial and irksome. It may not come naturally but it can be done. It has to be a conscious effort. You have to start by watching our thoughts and words, and speak with good purpose only.

Through a change in your reading habits and allowing your mind to be influenced by the right associations, you can accelerate the process and completely change your script to that of an enlightened millionaire. It is a small change in the initial condition that is required to create the 'Butterfly Effect'. And once the effect takes place, it becomes a part of your inner nature.

There can be no Change without Action

Thoughts and words have to manifest into action lest there will be no change. Moreover, action and events in the external world leave a far greater impact on your mind than thoughts and words.

Thoughts are the starting point. They are subtle but create the least impact. Once they manifest into words, they create a much greater impact on the mind. And once words manifest into action, they have the most powerful impact on our minds and the outer world.

To understand this point, let us take the example of an inventor; he thinks of a new invention or product. It is just a concept in his mind. He does not wish to pursue the idea further. It dies a natural death. If he decides to writes a paper on the subject and speak at a few seminars, it not only clarifies his thought process but also starts influencing the minds of others. Now if he takes action to create the new product, then it will impact his future in financial terms but will also leave an impact on those who use or associate with the product.

Actions, though a result of thoughts and words, can prove to be a more powerful instrument of change, as they have a greater impact on the script.

A huge number of people, who read the right kind of books, listen to tapes and attend seminars but take no action. They wish to acquire complete knowledge and eliminate risk before embarking on the process of wealth creation. That perfect situation never comes because what future beholds, no one knows—it is always full of uncertainties.

An educated mind can eliminate some eventualities but, "the fog of war will always remain." All successful commanders know when to act despite being provided with limited information on the enemy. Inaction certainly leads to defeat. The same is true in the world of finance.

If you do not act then you cannot make any money. There is saying: *"once you put your money in line, knowledge will come that much faster*." There is no faster way to rewrite the enlightened millionaire's script than to take action. There is no teacher like experience. Think big but start small. Learn to take a few successful steps before you can start to run.

Knowledge + Action = Wealth

Action is the key. Without action, all your knowledge turns to waste. Be bold and take action. Boldness has genius, power and magic.

Whatever your inspiration or dream—act on it. The most fundamental principle of wealth creation is to take action. No one can ever reach the stage of complete knowledge to overcome fear.

All wealth creators have to learn to manage fear. In every decision you take, there will be an element of uncertainty. There has to be a leap of faith as the information required for decision making is never adequate. Act, you must, in good faith and intelligence! Inaction will keep you tied to poverty.

Once you start taking action, your experience and confidence will increase. There is no better teacher than experience. A few successful steps will change your future. You will rewrite wealth script ten times faster with action.

Feelings make your Words and Actions Stronger

Words when spoken with feelings are a hundred times stronger than those spoken with no heart in them. Have you enjoyed a song that has been sung with passion? It takes a totally new dimension. The same is true for action when it is backed by positive emotion.

When there is joy in action, there is no burden on the task at hand. If the heart is not there, it becomes a tedious job. To rewrite your script your heart has to be in it. Without feelings, there will be no joy or beauty in your script. It will be very difficult to rewire.

Uncovering the power of your emotions will release a tidal wave of change in your life. When there is feeling of love in your words and actions, you will be transformed.

To understand your genius and passion, you have to be still. Through silent introspection, self-reflection and meditation you increase your self-awareness. As your self-awareness increases, you will understand what your heart really wants. Don't chase the artificial or what the world wants you to be. Be true to yourself and your inner beliefs and success will follow you.

Clarity of Purpose

There has to be clarity of purpose when rewriting your script or it will be unintelligible. If there is no clarity then you yourself will not be able to read your script, let alone understand it.

Firstly, there has to be a decision that resonates with: "*I will be an enlightened millionaire*." Then, you have to state your intention and commit it in writing. Writing your statement brings more clarity to your thought process.

Lastly, you have to announce it to the whole world that you are going to be an enlightened millionaire by a particular date—tell your friends, family and the whole world about your intentions. It will put pressure on you; instead it will keep you focused. You have to burn your bridges behind you to succeed. Without commitment, there is no clarity.

Goals are very critical to your success. They have to be clearly defined and practically achievable. To keep yourself balanced, you can record different goals in major areas of your life like health, relationships, intellectual, spiritual and financial goals. You have to write them, read them, see them and talk about them in every waking or dreaming moment of your life. You will then see your goals magically materialize into your life.

To become an enlightened millionaire you have to make a decision, state your intention and set goals. You have to live from your goals and think about them day and night.

Clarity and focus in your script will accelerate your pace of growth like nothing else. Can you imagine writing an article without a topic or a heading? The article will be confusing to the readers – it will be unintelligible. Similarly, without stating your goal and intention, your life script will be full of confusion.

To gain clarity you have to state your goals and put them in writing. You have to view and repeat these goals on a daily basis to stay on track and in focus. It looks simply but you will be surprised to learn that over 99% of the population has no stated goals and as a result, drift along in life. To be successful, you have to state your goals clearly and stay focused.

Being Congruent

There is a difference between a goal and an agenda: you can have a clearly stated goal but your hidden agenda can often sabotage that goal.

Our hidden agenda is normally driven by our ego, deep seated prejudices and value systems. Our hidden agendas are like saboteurs who are out to destroy our most well laid plans. We have to find these little saboteurs and convert them to our side.

To succeed you have to be congruent. You have to align your mind, body and spirit to a single purpose. Ask any top athlete. At the crucial point of winning-losing, they have their mind and body dissolves into one. There is no thought but only singularity of purpose. This singularity of purpose makes them champions.

The greatest loss of energy takes place because of attrition in the mind. When there is conflict of goals with our value system the script gets corrupted. We have to turn deep within ourselves to understand our hidden prejudices and value systems. We have to either bring in change to our inner attitudes or modify our goals to bring them into alignment with our core values. Without this, we will be working at cross purposes that will be deterrent to our success.

By little observation you can find out if there is a conflict within your mind and belief system.

People who complain of lethargy usually suffer from some kind of an inner conflict. One way to resolve such a conflict is through understanding the flow of energy. When everything is in alignment, there will be no noise and friction in the mind. If you are congruent, there will be explosion of energy within your system. Your script will then have clarity and sense of its purpose.

Transformational Change

Here we are not talking about increments in your script – we are talking of how you can achieve a quantum jump that can transform you instantly. It is transformational learning as against informational learning that is predominant in our educational system that defines our script.

Informational learning is passive; teachers talk and students listen. It is about memorization, examinations and grades. Teachers talk about subjects on which they have theoretical knowledge, but lack practical experience—such an education can never be inspirational.

Transformational learning is about self-discovery. The student is given an inspirational stimulus by a mentor who has traveled the path and has discovered the answers to the problems through his experience.

All the knowledge to become a millionaire is already within you. No one can teach you how to become rich. Someone can only inspire you to awaken every cell in your body that will cry out that you were born to be rich and free, and to live a life of abundance. It is your natural state.

Transformation occurs when the right stimulus is given to awaken what is inside us and our script changes instantaneously.

Mentors

The shortcut to transformational knowledge is to find a mentor; they are invaluable! They have travelled the path and they have the knowledge. They will stir you in their presence. A word of advice from them will transform you. It will be a life changing experience that no book, DVD or tape can provide.

Where can you find Mentors?

The truth is you cannot find a mentor until you are ready. The day you are ready a mentor will appear. A little preparation is required at your end to receive a mentor.

No one can inspire you until you are ready to be inspired. No one can change you until you desire the change. No one can make you rich until you want to be rich. When this happens, a mentor will appear in your life and take you forward in leaps.

There are mentors all around us but we don't see them because we are not mentally prepared for them. We associate ourselves with losers, time wasters, frivolous and non-productive people. How can we eject magnetic waves to attract successful people?

To gain some magnetic power, we have to initially force ourselves to the presence of people who emanate powerful doses of the magnetic energy we want. Association is a very powerful thing. If you associate with the right kind of people, you will be subjected to the right kind of energy fields. This will transform you. You will also become a magnet attracting the right kind of people. There is nothing new in it – it is the basic law of attraction.

"The soul attracts that which it secretly harbors, that which it loves, and also that which it fears. It reaches the height of its cherished aspirations. It falls to the level of its chastened desires – and circumstances are the means by which the soul receives its own." As a Man Thinketh by James Allen (1864 - 1912)

A mentor carries a hundred times stronger energy field. He can transform us to a different level instantly. However, we will receive the energy only once we are mentally prepared to accept the energy.

Thoughts have an energy that attracts like energy. A mentor will come to us when we are ready and not a day before that. We have to develop our thoughts (conscious and unconscious,) emotions, beliefs and actions to a certain level in order to attract the positive energy from a mentor.

If you study the lives of wealth creators, you will find they have been mentored not by one but several mentors at different periods of their lives. A mentor will not only fill the gaps in your knowledge but will inspire you to new levels of achievement, which you think is not possible. They will change your thought process and internal script.

Is it expensive to get mentors? Not necessarily. If you are serious and dedicated, you can get mentored for free. All masters take on assistants to do their 'grunt work,' so that they can leverage their time. You can volunteer to become their apprentice.

There is a Chinese proverb that goes like: "*A single conversation across the table with a wise man is worth a month's study of books.*" You can invite a mentor to a meal—it works like a charm.

The Millionaire Mind-set Scripts

We do not have to do anything spectacular to change our script to an 'enlightened millionaire's mindset,' but make small changes to alter the initial condition that can change the long-term trajectory of our lives.

T. Harv Eker in his brilliant book, Secrets of the Millionaire Mind, has written about wealth files or scripts for mastering the inner game of wealth. Some of the scripts are discussed in the succeeding paragraphs. These scripts are very powerful and can cause a 'Butterfly Effect.' You may apply some or all of them to change the outcome of your life. Please study these scripts carefully and start applying them gradually to your daily lives.

Rich people believe 'I create my life'. Poor people believe 'Life happens to me'

Enlightened millionaires take responsibility for their life and actions. They do not blame others when things go wrong. On the other hand, poor people think they are the victims and are experts at the 'blame game.' They blame the government, the economy, their bosses, friends and family when they fail. Blaming others for them is like a stress reducer. Complaining and justification are like pills they become addicted to.

You can either be rich or a victim—it depends on what script you choose. You slit your financial throat each and every time you choose to blame others. So choose to stay above the line. At the end of each day, carry out a complete debrief and write down each situation and how you handled it. This will dramatically change the outcome.

Rich people play the money game to win. Poor people play the money game not to lose

In sports, you can never win a game by playing defense; you have to be offensive and score if you have to win. I once saw a table tennis match—a really good player playing offence was matched against a defensive opponent and I had never seen a defensive player of his caliber. He was a virtual returning machine: he would stand twenty feet away from the table and continue returning the smashes from his opponent. It forced the smasher to make mistakes as he was the aggressor. The crowd cheered for the defensive player as he was unique or probably they identified with him. The aggressive player made several errors and lost points, but in the end, he won handsomely to the disappointment of the crowd.

I was in the Navy and in every war game we played offensive tactics to beat any purely defensive strategy. We also found that it was nearly ten times cheaper to build or buy an offensive weapon platform – like a missile boat or an aircraft launched missile – than to provide a credible defense against the threat.

The same holds true for the money game: truly rich people go on the offensive. Their goal is to acquire massive wealth. They shoot for the stars. Poor on the other hand, want to be comfortable. They never want to stick their necks out or pick up a challenge. They are always on the defensive, acting within their comfort zone. Security is of paramount concern to them. As a result, they never win and never get rich.

Rich people are committed to being rich. Poor people want to be rich

The number one reason most people don't get what they want is that they don't know what they want. Rich people are totally clear that they want wealth. They are unwavering in their mind and are fully committed to creating wealth. They will do whatever it takes, as long as it is moral, legal and ethical.

Based on the Laws of Attraction, the universe will conspire to help them achieve their goal because the message the rich send out to the universe is very clear – they want to be rich! The poor on the other hand, send out confused messages because of the negative wealth files. "What if I can make money and then lose it all? I'll be in the highest tax bracket and will have to give away half the money to the government—it's too much work. My health may suffer. I will have no time for my family. I'll never know if people like me for myself or my money...my kids could be kidnapped."

Most poor people want to be wealthy but have a confabulating script and a vague desire to be rich. This is why they do not succeed. The rich on the other hand have a script that is fully committed to creating wealth—devoid of any confusion whatsoever. They want to travel, have time on their hands, provide best possible things to their loved ones or help others and give money to charity. If you want to commit, then put your goals in writing and read them morning, evening and night. Announce your commitment to the entire world. Be congruent in thought, emotion and action. Clarity of purpose leads to success.

Rich people think big – Poor people think small

The difference between the rich and the poor is only a couple of zeros behind their incomes and net worth statements. It is as simple as that.

There is a saying: "Size of the question determines the size of the result." If you ask yourself a question: "Can I earn $30,000 doing this?" Then you will get the wrong result. If you ask yourself the question "How do I create or earn a million dollars?" Then your mind goes to work in a different direction. It wants to find a solution and works ceaselessly to find a satisfactory answer.

Most people fail to ask the big question – they choose to play small. They are frightened of failure and even scared to death of success. Our life is not about shrinking and feeling insecure—life is all about expansion and discovering our true worth. As we expand and liberate from our fears, our very presence liberates others from their small attitudes. Think big; there is no greatness in being small.

You will be a millionaire if you start thinking like a millionaire. Want to be a billionaire? Then learn to think big like a billionaire—it is all in the mind and beliefs you have.

Rich People focus on opportunities. Poor people focus on obstacles

Rich people see opportunities – poor people see obstacles. Rich people see potential growth – poor people see potential loss. Rich people focus on rewards – poor focus on risks. The mindset of the poor is, "It won't work." The mind-set of the rich is, "It will work because I will make it work."

What you focus on expands. If you focus on opportunities, they will expand. On the other hand, if you focus on obstacles, they will look insurmountable. If you want to be rich, focus on making, keeping and investing your money. If you want to be poor, focus on spending your money.

Rich people see an opportunity, jump on it and get richer. The poor look at the obstacles and keep preparing to overcome them. They never take action, which is why they lose.

Action always beats inaction. Rich people get started after understanding the risks; they make adjustments and corrections as they move along. If you want to be rich, focus on opportunities and take action.

Rich people admire other rich and successful people. Poor people resent rich and successful people

One of the surest ways to remaining poor is to resent the rich. Most poor people are conditioned to believe that one can't be both rich and spiritual simultaneously or be rich and a good person.

There can be nothing further from truth. To create wealth, certain human characteristics are needed. One has to be intelligent, hardworking, reliable, focused, determined, persistent and positive. Moreover, the person has to be a good communicator with a high degree of human skills and integrity. Without some of these skills coming into play, it is impossible to become rich in the first place.

There may be a few exceptions wherein people have become wealthy through ill-gotten means. However, in my experience such wealth never lasts for long. Seek inspiration from the enlightened rich who are, by far, some of the nicest people. They have reached where they are because of their expanded mental state and positive attitude to life.

Practice the Huna philosophy which states, '***Bless that which you want'***. Write a letter or an email to someone successful you admire. Tell them how much you admire and honor their achievement. You will develop an instant connection to success.

Rich people associate with positive, successful people. Poor people associate with negative or unsuccessful people

Easiest and fastest way to create wealth is through association. Be with the rich and learn how they became rich and mastered the game of money. 'If they can do it, I can do it'.

You must have heard the old adage: "Birds of a feather flock together." This is very true because most people earn within 20% of the average income of their closest friends. If you want to soar, fly with the eagles and don't get stuck swimming with the ducks.

Being in company of negatively minded people can be infectious. You can get measles of the mind. Instead of itching, you get bitching and instead of irritation, you get frustration.

It is not your job to reform negative people. You must keep away from them. Once you develop the positive energy field around you, they will get influenced by it but not before that.

In the initial stages, you must charge your energy field by hanging around with winners. Read biographies of the extreme rich and successful: Warren Buffet, Bill gates, Steve Jobs, Donald Trump, Andrew Carnegie and the likes.

Join clubs which the rich frequent. Identify friends and family who pull you down and stay away from them. Stop watching trash television and stay away from bad news that could potentially pollute the mind. **_Rich people hang around with winners. Poor hang around with losers_**_._ Never forget this basic principle.

Rich people are willing to promote themselves and their value. Poor people think negatively about selling and promotion

People who have issues with selling are usually broke – it's obvious. How can you create a large income in your business, or as a representative of one, if you aren't willing to let people know that you, your product, or your service exists? Even as an employee, if you are not willing to promote your virtues, someone who is willing will bypass you on the corporate ladder.

Poor have the fear of failure and rejection. They feel it is impolite to blow one's own trumpets. The world has so many products and services that nobody has the time for you or your product if you are not willing to step up and project yourself.

The poor have an attitude that makes them naively believe in their uniqueness. Hence, promotion is beneath them. Poor believe that because they are so special, someone will find them ultimately. They remain broke because of this attitude.

You may have the best talent and the product but no one will know of it if you are unwilling to promote. This is because everyone in the world has an information clutter and no time for you. You have to rise above the clutter and make yourself be heard.

Rich people are always excellent promoters. They know how to package their ideas, products and skills and they promote them with enthusiasm and passion. Robert Kiyosaki, author of the best-selling 'Rich Dad Poor Dad' series of books calls himself the "best-selling" and not the best writing author.

Every business depends on selling. Money is made only when something is sold in the market place. To become rich, you have to learn the art of promoting with 100 percent integrity. This can be done through courses in marketing and sales or reading books on the subject. People who shy away from this vital aspect cannot hope to amass wealth.

Rich people are bigger than their problems. Poor people are smaller than their problem

Poor people want to run away from problems – they don't want hassles and headaches. They will sweep them under the carpet or close their eyes like ostriches to wish them away. Problems have a habit of rebounding with a great vengeance. The more you try and avoid them...the poorer, broke and miserable they will keep you.

The secret to success is not to try to avoid or get rid of or shrink from your problems; the secret is to grow yourself so that you grow bigger than the problem.

The rich are problem solvers. They make money by identifying a problem and find a solution for it. People will pay money to solve their problems.

If by training you become level-10 problem solvers, do you think a level-5 problem will cause any worry or stress to you? The secret is to grow bigger than the problem.

The first step is to write down all the problems you are having in your life and then list actions to resolve them—this simple exercise will make your growth process to become bigger than your problems.

Your income will directly relate to the level of problem you are willing to solve. If you are an employee, you are solving a problem for your boss. You will get fired once you become a problem for the organization. If you are in business, you are solving problems for your clients. Be it servicing a car, providing plumbing services or pulling out a tooth. The quality of service and level of problem you are willing to solve will determine success of your business.

Rich people are excellent receivers. Poor people are poor receivers

For every giver there has to be a receiver, and for every receiver there must be a giver. One of the reasons why poor remain as poor is because they are poor receivers. They may or may not be good at giving but most certainly, they are poor receivers.

This holds true in every walk of life. To be loved, we have to know how to receive love. The universe has infinite abundance of wealth—it has to go somewhere. There are trillions of dollars floating around. If we are not ready to receive our share, it will go to someone who is willing to receive.

Being open to receiving is absolutely critical to creating wealth. There are times when money flows into our lives, we should accept the blessing of the universe gracefully and accept it as a gift.

Once you learn the art of receiving, you will become a money magnet and start attracting money.

Rich people choose to get paid on results. Poor people choose to get paid based on time

The thumb rule to becoming rich is: "***Never have a ceiling on your income***." *Poor people trade time for money. The problem with this strategy is that your time is limited. This means that you are breaking the fundamental rule of becoming rich which means having no ceiling on your potential income.*

Rich people prefer to get paid in results. If they run a business, they get paid from the profits. Alternately, they prefer to work on profit sharing, stock options or commissions.

In the financial world, rewards are proportional to the risk one is willing to take. What the poor do not realize is that job security comes at a price and that price is wealth. You can make a small start by requesting your employer to pay you partly based on the results. Another option is for you to set-up your own small business or consulting company, or to join a network marketing company and become result oriented.

Rich people think "both." Poor people think "either/or."

Rich people live in a world of abundance and poor people live in a world of limitations. Both live in the same physical world, but the difference is in their perspectives. Poor people think that either I can be rich or be spiritual.

Rich people think they can be both. Poor people think that either they can spend time with their families or work hard to become rich. Rich people think they can balance both.

Rich people believe "*You can have your cake and eat it too*." The middle-class people believe "*Cake is too rich, so I'll only have a small piece*." The script of the rich is to be creative and find ways for having "both."

The rich focus on their net worth; the poor on their working income

The vocabulary of the poor consists of: "How much I earn" or "How much I make." The rich, on the other hand, think of their net worth' and "How much profit I made." *The true measure of wealth is net worth, not working income.*

The words that write your script define your future. If you think in terms of 'earning' as opposed to 'net worth,' you will stay put in your job of trading time for money. ***Where attention goes, energy flows and results show***. So, focus your attention on the right script to increase your income. Simplify your life style to reduce your cost of living and invest the savings or surplus amount. Create a net worth statement and revise this statement every quarter to help analyze your progression.

Rich people manage their money well, Poor mismanage their money well

Rich people are good at managing their money though they are not necessarily smarter than the poor; they just have a different approach towards money.

This small difference in habit makes the biggest difference in the financial outcome of being rich or poor. Poor people either mismanage or they avoid the subject of money altogether. The excuse generally given is either, "It restricts our freedom" or "We don't have enough money or time to manage."

Nothing can be further from truth, because managing money allows financial freedom. ***The habit of managing your money is more important than the amount***. Until you learn how to handle what you've got, you are most likely not to get any more.

Rich people have their money work hard for them. Poor people work hard for their money

Most of us are programmed "*to work hard for money*." The rich on the other hand, reprogram themselves "**to make their money work hard for them**."

Working hard has never made anyone rich— working smart is the way to riches. The more your money works, the less you will need to work.

The definition of financial freedom is the ability to live the lifestyle you desire without having to work or rely on anyone else money. Therefore, to become free you will need to earn money without working. To do this you will need to create a passive income wherein money keeps flowing in whether you work or not.

The sources of passive income working for you can be either financial instruments like stocks, bonds, mutual funds or businesses working for you that are in confluence with: real estate, royalties from books, music or software, licensing your ideas, network marketing etc.

These will be discussed in depth later in the book. In simple terms: poor people work hard and spend all their money, which results in them having to work hard forever. Rich, on the other hand, work hard, save and then invest their money so they never have to work hard again.

The key is to change the money blueprint from immediate gratification to thinking long-term. Balance your spending on enjoyment today with investing in freedom tomorrow.

You will need to change your "Material gratification" files and replace them with "Financial freedom" files. Change your focus from "Active income" to "Passive income." List out strategies you can put to work to generate passive income.

Rich people act in spite of fear. Poor people let fear stop them

Fear freezes us to act and our well laid plans fail to manifest; thoughts lead to feelings, feelings lead to actions and actions lead to results.

We may have all the right knowledge but unless we act, there can be no wealth creation. *Action is a bridge between the inner and the outer world*. Rich and successful people have fear; they have doubts and worries like the rest of us but they do not allow these fears to stop them.

Poor people on the other hand, allow their fears to limit them. To change our scripts, we have to break the habit and make a conscious effort to act in spite of doubt, in spite of worry, in spite of uncertainty and discomfort. We have to learn to act even if we are not in a mood to do so.

Rich people constantly learn and grow whereas poor people think they already know.

*The three most dangerous words in English are "**I know that**." So how do you know if you know something? It is simple. If you live it, you know it. Otherwise, you heard about it, you read about it, or you talked about it, but you do not know about it. To know about it, you have to live it. If you are not really happy, there's a good chance you still have to learn about money, success and life.*

Poor people generally try and prove that they are right and they have got it figured out; it is just a stroke of bad luck or a temporary glitch that has them broke and struggling.

There is an excellent saying by Jim Rohn that makes perfect sense here: *"**If you keep doing what you've always done, you'll keep getting what you've always got".** If you are unsuccessful and not willing to change your life script or take the trouble to educate yourself, then you will keep getting the same results again and again. Someone rightly said, *"Definition of madness is to keep doing the same thing again and again and expect a different result."*

There is a constant need to learn and grow; everything alive is constantly changing. If a plant is not growing, it is dying. It is true for every organism including human beings. If you are not growing, then you are dying.

Author and philosopher, Eric Hoffer, has rightly said, *"Learners shall inherit the world while the learned will be beautifully equipped to live in a world that no longer exists."* This means that if you are not constantly learning and growing you will be left behind.

Poor people usually complain that they do not have either the time or the money to get educated—these are plain excuses. The only thing normally lacking is the commitment to learn and change. Rich people, on the other hand, relate to Benjamin Franklin's famous quote: *"If you think education is expensive, try ignorance."*

Poor people seek advice from relative and friends who are equally clueless. This keeps them entangled in the web of poverty. The most expensive advice you can ever receive is free advice from an ignorant person.

Rich, on the other hand, continuously read books and attend seminars to improve the skills and strategies they need to accelerate their income, manage their money and then invest it effectively. They learn the game of money from those who are the masters in the field and have success become a corollary of it.

Your income is directly related to your inner growth, which includes: financial, emotional and spiritual IQ. You must commit to your growth and consider hiring personal coaches to keep you focused and on track in the various aspects of your life, including health.

The outer world is merely a manifestation of your inner world. There are outer laws of money that entail: business knowledge, money management and investment strategies.

Equally important are the inner laws, or the script that defines you as a person. It is not enough to be at the right place at the right time. You have to be the right person in the right place at the right time.

Fear, which is the biggest enemy of wealth creation, can – to a large extent – be controlled by expanding our financial, emotional and spiritual intelligence. The internal change in the script is critical before we can learn about the outer laws of wealth creation which in comparison are very easy to master. Once the internal transformation is complete, there is no force on earth that can stop you from becoming a millionaire.

Driving Force behind Wealth Creation

What drives you to create wealth is a very important factor that will determine your success. Deeper your motivation, stronger will be your foundation to create wealth.

If your desire to create wealth is motivated by external factors – such as buying a luxury car, going on a holiday, or moving into a larger house – then they are not formidable enough to take you very far. There is nothing wrong with these desires, but they can be satisfied soon enough. Money can buy you things, but not happiness.

Similarly, if acquiring wealth is motivated by greed or fear then it will not bring you happiness. These motivations are non-supportive and therefore, not deep enough to create sustained wealth.

To create long-term wealth, you have to be driven by an inner drive that is hard to satisfy. These may include: search for freedom from a job you do not like, to pursue your passion, your hobbies and sports. One of the great internal motivations can be the pursuit of personal growth including health.

The strongest innate motivation is the desire to help others—elevate them from their sufferings or teach them, using your own example as muse, how to create enlightening wealth. By pursuing a deeper cause, you will not only bring about transformational change within yourself but also the ones around you.

There are always challenges in creating wealth. It is easier to overcome those challenges once you motivation level is deeper than superficial.

Certain actions and changes in your everyday life may act as stimulus to understanding your deeper motivation. Firstly, give more value than you take from others: when you give value to others, you improve your own life. Wealth created by exploiting others never lasts long, and does it provide any internal happiness.

There should be a high level of integrity in your everyday actions. You cannot cheat your way into any meaningful wealth. Your mind is a great powerhouse; keep it pure and creative. Don't waste your energy in the pursuit of wealth through shortcuts and by causing harm to others.

The deeper and nobler your cause, greater will be your wealth. Such wealth will also provide you with inner happiness and peace.

Final Thoughts

Inner transformation always precedes wealth creation. I failed in my first few attempts at business not because of lack of hard work or effort, but because I was not adequately mentally prepared for business. My wealth grew in proportion to the inner change that was taking place within me.

Awareness of the inner principles of wealth creation is one small step and transformation will not happen overnight; combing action and experience will speed up that process. Constant education, associating with the right groups of people, and deep reflection will play a huge role if you wish to progress on the path of acquiring a wealthy mindset. Try and seek mentors at each stage of your growth—it will hasten your growth process. Make small changes in your life and observe the butterfly effect play out.

Whether you are an employee, self-employed, an investor or in business—applying the principles enunciated this book will help you grow financially. Slowly but surely you will embrace abundance which is your birth right.

The purpose of this book will be served if it helps in educating and help morph enlightened people who create wealth the right way, preserve wealth the right way and ultimately, use their wealth for the greater good of humanity. This process leads to seeking a higher purpose in life and its fulfillment. I hope and pray that to some extent, that purpose is served. If you have read to this point, I thank you with gratitude in my heart and hope you succeed in creating true wealth that helps not only you and your family but entire humanity.

If you liked the book and gained some knowledge that will be useful to you in life, then please leave an honest review to help others find this book. It will be a small effort on your part, but an act of charity that may help in changing few lives for the better. We thank you in advance for your help.

This book is about fundamental principles of wealth creation that can be applied to any business or investing strategy. At Wealth Creation Academy, we teach multitude ways to generate passive income, which includes: real estate investing, digital publishing, affiliate marketing, multi-level marketing and investing in forex, commodities, and shares by copying experienced traders that need very little of time.

You may like to get started with some of the strategies depending on your budget and time.

Other Books by the Authors

Praveen Kumar has authored several bestselling books. Please visit his website **http://praveenkumarauthor.com/** for more information

About the Authors

Praveen Kumar was abandoned by his father at the age of fourteen and joined the Navy at tender age of fifteen where education, roof and free food were guaranteed.

In order to understand the root cause of suffering he turned towards philosophy and religion. After 10 years of soul searching and meditation he understood that 'life is 'and material and spiritual world are closely interwoven. You cannot live in one without the other.

Praveen was highly successful in the Navy, where he successfully commanded submarines, sailed around the world in a yacht and received gallantry award for his contribution to the Navy.

Despite his success in the Navy, Praveen realized that lack of financial security for his family was one of key root causes of his suffering, resulting from his childhood deprivation. To improve his financial standing, Praveen took pre-mature retirement from the Navy to build his financial future through investing in Real Estate. The decision to educate on financial matters paid off, and today he and his wife are comfortably retired on six-figure passive income.

His aim is to help others create wealth in an enlightened way and empower them to live a healthy and happy life. He dedicates his time to write books and articles on financial and spiritual matters.

Prashant graduated with distinction from Auckland University as a computer engineer and later completed his MBA from the world's leading institution - INSEAD. During his successful corporate career, he worked for the most reputable consulting firms in the world - BCG & Deloitte - and represented New Zealand on Prime

Minister-led trade missions to South East Asian countries.

After successfully generating income through his passive investments in property and stocks, Prashant decided to team up with his father to help people transform their lives through the leverage of financial education.

Their website http://wealth-creation-academy.com/ is devoted to teaching people how to create Multiple Streams of Passive Income through investing in real estate, online marketing and creating digital products